Original title:
The Ocean's Whispering Heart

Copyright © 2025 Creative Arts Management OÜ
All rights reserved.

Author: Rory Fitzgerald
ISBN HARDBACK: 978-1-80587-292-4
ISBN PAPERBACK: 978-1-80587-762-2

Reflection in the Gentle Surf

Waves roll in with a playful splash,
Seagulls dive down for a quick dash.
Sandcastles made with a bucket and grin,
Watch as the tide says, "Not today, kin!"

Children giggle, their joy in the air,
A crab in a tux, what a sight rare!
Laughter erupts with each funny fall,
As slip-slidey feet dance, calling us all.

The Spirit of the Coral Reef

Fish wear bow ties at the coral ball,
Jellyfish waltz with a graceful sprawl.
Starfish applaud with their multiple hands,
While clams gossip softly about beachy bands.

An octopus juggles shells with great zeal,
Mollusks whisper secrets, oh what a deal!
A turtle in shades cruised by with a wink,
"Time to chill out, don't you think?"

Serenade of the Seabreeze

The wind's a joker, tickling my nose,
With seaweed swaying, it takes off my clothes.
A dolphin sings tunes we can't quite catch,
While the crabs hold a dance-off, what a match!

Lighthouses chuckle, their beams shining bright,
As the sun plays peek-a-boo, a golden delight.
Footprints in sand write notes to the tide,
"Come dance with us, we've nothing to hide!"

Horizon's Giggle

The sun dips low, throwing colors a'plenty,
While waves tease the shore, oh so gently.
A hermit crab races, but slips on its shell,
The ocean laughs hard, it's under its spell.

Kites soar above, like fish in the sky,
A puff of wind makes a toddler cry.
But giggles return as they chase a bright kite,
Playing with shadows that dance in twilight.

Swaying Kelp

In the dance of green, they do twirl,
With fish in hats, making a whirl.
A seaweed party, what a sight,
Even crabs join in, feeling just right.

Jellyfish float like balloons from a fair,
While octopuses juggle with flair.
The current's a DJ, spinning tunes,
Making waves move like wild buffoons.

Swaying Hearts

Fish play Cupid with their little arrows,
While clams gossip like old sea sparrows.
Starfish declare their love with each star,
And dolphins swim by, humbling bazaar.

With every splash, a giggle erupts,
As turtles take selfies, feeling grown-ups.
Seashells pass notes wrapped in a swirl,
In this quirky whirlpool, love's just a whirl.

Breezes That Bring Memories

The breeze carries tales from afar,
Of silly crabs in a beach-side bazaar.
Seashells giggle; the sand tickles toes,
As laughter bubbles where the foam flows.

Each puff of air sings a ballad true,
Of mermaid parties, and fish in a stew.
The scent of salt brings back the past,
We chuckle and dance, making memories last.

A Rhapsody Under Waves

Beneath the waves, there's a concert grand,
With bass that boom and squeaky bands.
Clownfish try to steal the show,
While sea cucumbers sway, feeling the flow.

Giant squids play the hoedown beat,
While seahorses tango, oh what a feat!
They groove to the rhythm hidden below,
Where silliness blooms, and the giggles grow.

The Lure of the Distant Blue

In the distance, the blue calls aloud,
With winking sea sprites, and giggling crowds.
The horizon beckons with a wink and a nod,
As jellyfish prance like they're the gods.

Waves tease us, just a little bit shy,
While clams make wishes, oh my, oh my!
Dive into fun, let worries just float,
In the lure of the deep, we'll dance like a boat.

Veil of Misty Horizons

A seagull cawed, then slipped on a pie,
Riding high winds as the jellyfish fly.
The lighthouse blinks, it's surely confused,
Does it guide boats or help them get snoozed?

Barnacles gossip on the side of the boat,
"Did you see Dave? He forgot how to float!"
The waves wave back, they're tickling your toes,
While crabs throw parties in their sand-colored clothes.

Beneath the Glistening Surface

Fish wear sunglasses, flashing their scales,
While dolphins tell jokes and swap silly tales.
An octopus dances, all arms in the air,
"Join in!" he shouts, "It's a tentacle affair!"

A clam thinks of pearls, but prefers to just yawn,
While the starfish sleeps, saying, "I'm a star gone!"
Bubbles are giggling as they float up to play,
Underwater humor? It's shellfish, they say!

Where the Sea Meets the Sky

Seagulls on scooters zoom overhead,
"Who wants a snack?" one chirps, full of dread.
The waves shout jokes as they crash on the shore,
"You're always salty, but never a bore!"

A beach ball rolls off to join in the fun,
"Catch me if you can!" it gleefully runs.
Sandcastles giggle as the tide comes to play,
"Don't wash us away, we're kings for a day!

Vessel of Tranquil Depths

Mermaids complain, "These shells are a mess!
They just don't fit, this ain't even a dress!"
While turtles are laughing, rolling on the floor,
"Who knew such fun would come from the shore?"

A whale hums tunes that tickle the seals,
"Do you hear that sound? It's my new 'whale' of deals!"
The fish throw a bash, it's a party at dark,
Revving their engines, and singing with spark.

Below the Surface

Fish in suits, they swim with pride,
Underwater parties that no one hides.
Twirling seaweed, a dance so slick,
They invite the crabs, it's quite the trick.

A jellyfish wearing a bowtie bright,
Winks at a clam, oh what a sight!
Starfish clap, with applause they cheer,
For a fish who can rap, drawing quite near.

Above the Pain

Seagulls turn, they squawk and dive,
Making jokes about the waves that thrive.
A dolphin stuck in a sunken shoe,
Laughs as he lets out a bubbly 'moo!'

Cranky crabs throw a tantrum fit,
When they trip on a net, oh what a hit!
Octopus juggling the beach ball high,
Shouting, "Catch me, or at least try!"

A Sea Glass Tale

Once was a bottle that danced away,
Caught in a wave, it decided to play.
Then it shattered, oh what a fate,
Turning cool glass into treasures straight.

A mermaid's mirror, reflective and green,
Used to brush hair, oh what a scene!
Shrimp wear it proudly, a shiny crown,
With laughter and bubbles, they never frown.

Dancers on the Shimmering Sea

Starfish spinning in their ball gowns bright,
While bubbles bob along in delight.
The sun joins in, wearing shades of gold,
As sea turtles dance, so graceful, so bold.

A whale in the back does the limbo sway,
While the fishes throw seaweed, come what may.
With laughter and splashes, the tide joins the fun,
In this salty soirée under the sun.

An Ocean of Emotion

Waves crashing hard, like a toddler's fit,
While starfish giggle, not losing their wit.
Seahorses trotting with whimsical flair,
They hide their own giggles behind their long hair.

Anemones blush, tickled by brush,
As surfboards glide in a ripple-rush.
With every splash, there's laughter in sight,
In this watery world, everything's light.

Dance of the Tide's Caress

The waves do cha-cha on the shore,

They giggle and splash, then ask for more.

Seagulls throw shade while doing the twist,

While shells whisper tales that we can't assist.

The crabs in their pinstripe pants groove,

Doing the moonwalk, they make us move.

Starfish play tag, they sure are spry,

Instructions from clams? We can only sigh.

Whispers from the Coral Abyss

Bubbles are burbling, like laughter at play,
The fish tell each other, 'It's a fine day!'
Turtles stumble, forgetting their grace,
While seaweed dances, just keep up the pace.

Octopus juggles, but drops a few fish,
His buddies all laugh, it's quite the swish!
Crabs crack out jokes, in their crabby style,
With a pinch and a wink, they stay for a while.

The Deep's Soft Serenade

The jellyfish float, like balloons in the air,
Wobbling softly, without a care.
Sharks fashion hats, in a dapper parade,
While dolphins just whistle, their joy displayed.

Clownfish linger, with chuckles galore,
Swapping fish stories that never get bore.
Anglerfish grins with a light in his face,
"Who's the best fisherman? Let's pick up the pace!"

Lullabies of the Seafoam

Foamy whispers tickle the toes,

Mollusks tell secrets that nobody knows.

Gulls crack a joke, then fly off in haste,

While whales hum tunes, utterly chaste.

Sand dollars play cards, they're quite the lot,

Counting their wins, in the warm sunspot.

Clams clap in rhythm, with shells held so tight,

Jesting about snacks in the soft moonlight.

Shadows in the Aquatic World

Fish wear hats, quite a sight,
Trying to dance, with all their might.
Jellyfish float, in a silly parade,
Bubble-blowing antics, never fade.

Crabs in tuxedos, scuttle with flair,
Tickled by seaweed, without a care.
An octopus juggling, with such grace,
Laughing so hard, he's lost the race.

An Ocean's Lullaby

Seahorses sing, in a harmony sweet,
While clams tap their shells, to the beat.
Dolphins do flips, in a giggly splash,
As sea turtles munch, in a slow, calm crash.

Starfish are stars, on a sandy stage,
Reading their scripts, from a water page.
Waves whisper jokes, from afar,
As the moon winks down, like a movie star.

Between Waves and Whispers

Mermaids gossip, with tails in the breeze,
While sea cucumbers shake, if you please.
Underwater parties, with bubbles and cheer,
Every fish laughing, as they chug root beer.

Turtles in ties, holding a dance,
Moving in circles, they prance and prance.
A starry night's glow, with fishy delights,
They celebrate life, beneath twinkly lights.

Call of the Siren's Song

Sirens are singing, but what do they mean?
Are they trying to charm, or just eat ice cream?
With a wink and a wave, they beckon the brave,
But their secret's revealed, it's a crab rave!

Fish in tuxedos, they shimmy and shake,
Caught in a current, but make no mistake.
They tango and spin, 'til the bubbles arise,
In water so warm, beneath starlit skies.

Tides of Silent Stories

Waves giggle as they crash and splash,
Squirrels in shells having a mad dash.
Fish wear hats to dance on the sand,
Seagulls squawking like they've lost their band.

Crabs holding meetings at the moonlit shore,
Debating the best way to settle a score.
Jellyfish disco under starlit wraps,
While starfish play poker, betting on naps.

A fish in a bowtie sings out a tune,
Dancing with seaweed under the moon.
Mussels discuss their holiday plans,
As barnacles gossip, all waving their hands.

At high tide they gather, it's quite the scene,
A beach party where they eat jellybean.
And when the tide rolls back, they all disappear,
Leaving just echoes of laughter, I hear.

Murmurs Beneath the Surface

Bubbles chuckle as they float away,
Dolphins flipping like they're in a ballet.
Turtles wear glasses to read the tide,
While octopuses hide their dance moves with pride.

Crabs are the influencers of the reef,
Posing for selfies, oh what a belief!
Sea cucumbers are just in disguise,
Saying they're the stars, oh how time flies!

Mussels munching on seaweed stew,
Claiming it's gourmet, consider it new.
Anemones giggle at the seaweed's plight,
While narwhals play tag in the dim light.

The current whispers secrets of good cheer,
As jellyfish join in, spinning here and there.
Their tentacles waving like arms in the air,
Making quite the stir, with fish everywhere!

The Call of Distant Shores

A clam called for help, said it's lost its song,
Said seashells were singing just a bit wrong.
Waves dashed off giggling, with the tides' delight,
As sand dollars flipped, dancing through the night.

Seagulls tell tales of sea-sick old ships,
As mermaids swim past with salty sweet sips.
Crabs scribble notes in the warm, wet sand,
Leaving behind secrets of the sea and land.

Turtles racing, in a shell of a hurry,
While fish swim in circles, causing a flurry.
The moody seaweed sways, feeling quite grand,
Swaying to music it made with a band.

And when the moon shines, it's time for a show,
Who knew that a minnow could dance, oh so slow?
With washed-up treasures and stories to share,
The waves hold laughter, if you choose to care.

Secrets of the Blue Abyss

Deep down where the bubbles giggle and glow,
A walrus holds court, with a comedic show.
Clownfish in costumes, all dressed up in flair,
Making the eels laugh as they twirl through the air.

Starfish play games of tickle and chase,
While oysters cheer loudly from their cozy place.
A conch shell pretends it's a trumpet so grand,
Playing polka beats, the best in the land.

Garden of coral, a brilliant display,
Where sea horses frolic, it's a barn dance heyday.
Dancing with krill, in a waltz that's just right,
While lobsters sport shades on this vibrant nightlife.

As the currents they swirl, in a joyful embrace,
Making mischief with bubbles, an aquatic chase.
The secrets they hold, full of laughter and thrill,
Are whispers of joy in the deep, never still.

Beneath the Ocean's Skin

Bubbles rise like laughter,
Fish giggle in the tide,
Coral reefs wear sunglasses,
Seaweed dances with pride.

Crabs play tag on the sand,
Starfish cheer from their spots,
A clam's hiding with a grin,
While sea sponges tie knots.

Jellyfish float, quite silly,
Waves tickle with a splash,
Octopuses play piano,
In a symphonic mash.

The tide rolls in, full of glee,
Shells whisper jokes to the shore,
While dolphins tell tall tales,
Of treasure hunts and more!

The Siren's Unseen Wail

Siren sings with a smirk,
Her notes make sailors dance,
But under a veil of sea foam,
She giggles with mischance.

With fins like sparkling fringe,
She splashes water with flair,
Mermaids fight for the spotlight,
In a splashy, silly dare.

Ships go down, but just for laughs,
As they chase her song of cheer,
"Come taste the salty snacks!" she croons,
"Don't worry, there's nothing to fear!"

With a wink and a wild flip,
She marches through the blue,
While fish cover their ears with glee,
For her tunes are quite askew!

Dancer of the Deep

Beneath the waves, she twirls,
Anemones sway with grace,
A lazy seal joins the fun,
In this underwater race.

Her fins are like confetti,
Sparkling under the sun,
Sea turtles cheer her on,
As she spins and she runs.

Bubble parties are a blast,
They light up the dark sea,
With laughter and some flippers,
Who wouldn't want to be free?

With a twirl and a flip flop,
She charms the creatures near,
Dancing deep in the ocean,
Where everyone drinks up cheer!

Shadows of the Forgotten Atlantis

In Atlantis where laughter hides,
Merfolk share their old tales,
With crumbling ruins as stages,
Echoes of giggly gales.

Treasure chests filled with candy,
And bubbles that fizz so bright,
The shadows dance like silly ghosts,
In the moon's whitish light.

They toast to the sunken city,
With drinks made of seaweed juice,
"More parties!" they chant delighted,
"Let's bring forth the fishy roots!"

With tridents held high in jest,
They invite all to their feast,
In the depths of the forgotten,
Where humor never ceased!

A Paddle's Embrace

In waves that giggle, I try to steer,
My paddle spins, now I'm in a cheer.
A fish jumps high, does a silly flip,
Splashing my snack, oh what a trip!

The seagulls laugh as I wade near,
Stealing my chips, oh how rude, dear!
I wave my hand, they take to the air,
I chase my snacks, but find just despair!

My boat is rocking, a dance in the sun,
Each wobble is funny; oh, isn't this fun?
A crab on the shore, he beckons me close,
But who needs crabs when I have this toast?

In laughter and splashes, the day rolls away,
From fishes with flippers to ducklings at play.
With a paddle in hand and a smile so wide,
The ocean's a jester; let the humor ride!

Cradle of the Ocean's Children

Tiny shells laugh on the sandy shore,
They sing sweet songs, begging for more.
A jellyfish glows and dances with glee,
While crabs play tag, running wild and free!

Gulls overhead with a mocking squawk,
They join the party; it's quite the shock!
I try to catch one—oh what a laugh,
They drop my sandwich, my lunch, from the staff!

Mermaids swim by, with a wink and a wave,
In their bubbly laughter, they misbehave.
"Join us! Join us!" they splash and they twirl,
But I think I'll stay dry; I prefer to swirl!

In this cradle of giggles, the tides softly tease,
Nature's own humor is meant to please.
With seaweed as hair and dolphins in play,
I'll cherish these moments, let joy lead the way!

Enchanted by the Seafoam

The seafoam whispers secrets, oh so bright,
It tells silly tales that dance in the light.
A seal pops up with a fishy grin,
"Bet you can't catch me!"—let the games begin!

Waves tickle my toes as I laugh and sway,
Playing hide and seek with a crab at midday.
The seaweed is tangled, a green, leafy mess,
It wraps 'round my legs, oh what a distress!

Giggling rays of sunshine above,
Join in the fun, as we play and hug.
A mermaid winks, her laughter bright,
"Let's race the tide; it's a silly sight!"

In joy and in chaos, the sea fools around,
With giggles and splashes, we're joyfully wound.
The foam is a friend; with laughter, it flows,
In the heart of the sea, where silliness grows!

Driftwood Dreams

I found a piece of driftwood, oh so fine,
It looked like a sword, so I claimed it mine.
A pirate I am, in my dreams so grand,
With seashells for treasure, oh this is the plan!

But the wood rolls away, as if it can see,
"No pirate here, come chase after me!"
I dive and I splash; I make quite the scene,
While the seagulls chuckle, so mean and so keen!

A surfboard turtle rides by with a laugh,
"Join our surfing class, just be a half!"
With waves crashing down and my heart full of glee,
This driftwood saga is the best memory!

As sunlight dips low in a blush of pink hue,
I bask in the giggles of this oceanic brew.
With driftwood dreams and laughter without end,
I'll cherish these moments, 'till the tide we amend!

The Pulse of Salted Air

Waves come in, and so do seagulls,
Stealing fries, oh what fun that pulls!
The tide rolls in, then rolls right out,
Guess it's time for a sandcastle drought.

Buckets and shovels, we march with pride,
But crabs sneak up, oh how they glide!
Sand in my sandwich, not quite a treat,
I laugh and I snack on my sandy feat.

Sunburns dance on a skin so pale,
I thought I was tough, but boy, I sail!
Watermelon slices, sticky and sweet,
But a bee flew in, now I have to retreat!

Surfboards waiting, but I'll just sit,
Watching the pros, I'm okay with a split.
The salty breeze whispers funny tales,
Of belly flops and jellyfish fails.

Fantasies of the Ocean Floor

Octopuses dreaming of fashion and flair,
Dressed in shells, they'll give quite a scare!
Starfish in sequins, they dance like a pro,
Twirling and giggling, under the sea glow.

A crab with a hat, what a sight to behold,
He sips on a cocktail, so brave and so bold!
Mermaids are laughing, their hair all a mess,
"Who brought the snacks?" they shout, in distress!

Fish schools gossiping, they swim to and fro,
"Did you hear about Barnacle Bill's new yellow glow?"
Sharks trade their stories of heroic, wild quests,
While oysters start fretting, "We're late for the fest!"

Deep down below, where the seaweed does sway,
Sea horses boogie, come join their ballet!
With bubbles of laughter, they spin round and round,
Underwater antics, where joy can be found.

Sentiments of Sea Glass

A bottle washed up from a day long past,
Filled with nostalgia, it rolls and it's fast!
What secrets it holds, love notes or a dare?
The sea shrieks with laughter, "It's junk, I swear!"

Shards of glass sparkle, like jewels on the sand,
Looking for treasures, oh isn't it grand?
With toes in the water, I spot a fine piece,
"Is this a lost ticket for oceanic cheese?"

Beachcombers gather, their finds in a row,
One claims a shell, while another says "No!"
A fish in a bottle, just swimming around,
"What's the fuss, folks? I'm just here to clown!"

Yet each little trinket carries a tale,
Of summer fun, and some epic fail!
I chuckle alone, with my treasures in hand,
As the waves keep on whispering, ever so grand.

Anemone's Gentle Breath

Anemones sway, tickling fish by the fin,
"Come play with us, let the fun begin!"
They smile with colors, oh such a delight,
Puffing and laughing, what a silly sight.

Clownfish parade with their ruffled-up hair,
Wiggling and giggling, without a care!
One trips on a coral, what a goofy flail,
The seaweed erupts in a fit of whale-tail.

Jellyfish bobbing, doing howdy-do's,
With stings that are ticklish, a giggly muse!
"Watch your step, friends," one squeaks with a grin,
"Or you'll end up dancing on slippery skin!"

Whirlpools and whirlwinds of laughter unite,
With jellybeans spilling, oh what a sight!
Bubble parties bloom, under stars shining bright,
In the gentle embrace of a sea-full delight.

Love Letters to the Sea

Dear sea, you're quite a tease,
With waves that tickle my knees.
You splash my face with salty grace,
And laugh as I stumble with ease.

Oh, how you play hide and seek,
With tides that change like hideous chic.
You sent me a message in a bottle,
It said, 'Don't take a dip; it's too bleak!'

Your crabs wear tiny little hats,
While dolphins plan their acrobatic prats.
I tried to surf, fell in with a splash,
Now I'm the sea's biggest laughing brat!

So here's my love, oh salty friend,
Till the very last wave, may this fun never end!
I'll write you more letters, you quirky fiend,
In this playful sea dance, our bonds will mend.

Between Distant Shores

Between beaches, dreams collide,
A seagull swoops, and off I glide.
With sand in my shoes, I trip and roll,
Lost in laughter, that's my goal!

I sent a postcard to a whale,
Told him my jokes, none could curtail.
He just hooted, bubble-blown,
Guess he didn't like my funny tales!

The tide brought in a pair of shorts,
With a note saying, 'Nice of you to court!'
I waved goodbye to a floating shoe,
The sea's comedy shows always renew!

Between waves and smiles, we unite,
Where silliness comes with every bite.
So here's to laughter, my distant friend,
May the fun keep rolling, with no end!

Dunes of Dreams

In the dunes, I built a tower,
Each grain of sand, a silly power.
But too much wind swept it away,
Now I'm a sandcastle buffet!

I found a crab with a funky hat,
Dancing solo, imagine that!
I joined him and we did a jig,
The other critters laughed, that's our gig!

Sandy toes and a sunburned nose,
Guess I shouldn't pose too close.
With sunscreen thick, I look quite funny,
Like a lobster wrapped in golden honey!

So here in these dunes, I'll take my stand,
With salty dreams and this wacky band.
Let's laugh and play till the stars appear,
In this merry madness, let's shed a cheer!

Lighthouses of Lost Souls

Oh lighthouse, standing tall and bright,
You guide the ships with all your might.
But what about me, lost on the shore?
I'm just looking for snacks, nothing more!

I wrote a joke to pass the time,
Gulls squawked back, their version of rhyme.
A buoy chimed in with a pun so grand,
'Tide you up, buddy, it's all unplanned!'

Navigating waves like a bumpy ride,
I slip and slide, but take it in stride.
My compass spins with mirth and jest,
In this ocean playground, I feel so blessed!

So, dear lighthouse, keep shining true,
While I dance with fish in my water shoe.
Together we'll laugh at all things nautical,
In this silly boating life, oh so magical!

Tides of Silent Secrets

Waves dance like fish in a fancy ball,
Their wiggly moves make everyone fall.
Seagulls in tuxedos, strut and preen,
While crabs pinch toes, the silliest scene.

A starfish in shades, lounging with flair,
Sipping on seaweed, without a care.
The seashells gossip, oh what a mess,
Who wore it best? Now that's the stress!

Jellyfish giggle, floating around,
Tickling dolphins, without making a sound.
Octopus chefs, flipping fish with a twist,
Running the kitchen, they sure can't miss!

As the sun sets low, it's time for a show,
Crabs clap their claws, putting on quite a glow.
The tide rolls back, but the humor's in sight,
Underwater laughter, oh what a delight!

Beneath the Blue Embrace

In depths of blue where the clownfish play,
They tell goofy jokes, brightening the day.
Anemones wiggle, tickling tails,
While turtles rock out, telling tall tales.

The anglerfish shines, but it's just for a laugh,
With a light under chin, he's the life of the staff.
A snail with a shell that's decked out in flair,
Claims he's the speedster, but who really cares?

The crabs play poker, cards flapping in glee,
Bluffing right under the shadowed sea tree.
With bubbles of laughter swelling and bright,
The silly sea life dances into the night.

As the moonlight sparkles, it's time for a giggle,
Underwater parties, where creatures all wiggle.
With fishy confetti and seaweed garlands,
They dance till dawn, like joy on the strands!

Echoes of the Deep

Echoes call out in a puzzly way,
As fish whisper secrets of another day.
A dolphin named Dave, with a wink and a grin,
Teaches sea turtles how to do spins.

Barnacles grumble about breakfast time,
While shrimp do the cha-cha, oh so sublime.
An octopus juggles with jelly, oh dear!
His eight arms are busy, it's quite the career!

Whales sing their tunes, like a pop concert,
But dolphins just laugh, "Is anyone hurt?"
With bubbles that burst, and seaweed confetti,
They dance through the currents, all bright and ready.

In the deep, it's a hoot, where laughter flows free,
Chasing the currents, happy as can be.
With giggles and gurgles from creatures galore,
The ocean's a comedy, we all can explore!

Currents of Lost Lore

Old tales drift by on the backs of the waves,
Of pirates and mermaids, and treasure caves.
But here comes a lobster, with stories to share,
Of sassy adventures that float in the air.

With a wink and a nod, she's spinning a yarn,
'Twas a crab named Fred who could really charm!
He danced on the sand and sang with delight,
While seahorses twirled through the shimmering light.

The wise old sea turtle, with tales of the past,
Winks at the starfish, who's confused and aghast.
"Did you really see a fish wearing a hat?"
"Of course!" chirps a shrimp, "And he danced like that!"

As the tide rolls out, the stories encore,
Chasing the waves, forever to soar.
With laughter and lore, the sea holds its art,
A treasure of fun, straight from its heart!

Secrets in the Brine

Fish wear hats to catch a breeze,
While crabs moonwalk with awkward ease.
Mermaids giggle, they hide their tails,
Telling tales of their failed sails.

Dolphins dance with goofy glee,
Waving to jellyfish on a spree.
Seagulls squawk, they think they're cool,
But they've never been to seagull school.

Barnacles gossip upon the rocks,
Playing games with sunken clocks.
Turtles race, but always lose,
And blame it on their heavy shoes.

So dive in deep, and plumb the jokes,
Where bubbles burst and laughter pokes.
In the salty depths, we'll find our fun,
Where secrets live beneath the sun.

Lullabies of the Rising Tides

The waves sing softly, oh so sweet,
While starfish tap dance on their feet.
Seahorses strut in tiny boots,
Twirling tales in kelp-filled hoots.

Crabs hold concerts with funky beats,
As clams clap shells to mark their feats.
The gentle lapping makes you grin,
As fish swim by, all wearing fin.

Octopuses play hide and seek,
With jiggles and wobbles, they look so meek.
Their eight arms flail in silly plight,
Crafting shadows in drifting light.

So rock-a-bye, there's so much fun,
In watery realms where folks do run.
As tides rise up to spin and sway,
With sleepy laughs to close the day.

Colors of the Sunlit Sea

The sea's a canvas, wild and bright,
With polka dots in morning light.
Coral's pink, and laughter's blue,
Bubblegum waves all laugh and woo.

A squid paints rainbows wide and free,
While starfish share their mystery.
The sardines shimmer, dance and prance,
As shells join in the underwater dance.

Yellow sunbeams tickle the foam,
Making every fish feel at home.
With splashes bright, and frisky leaps,
It's a party where no one sleeps.

Each inch a story, each wave a thrill,
Come ride the colors, if you will.
In this laughter, wildly profound,
The sea paints joy—ever found!

The Soul of the Sailor

A sailor's hat is full of dreams,
His pockets jingle with shiny schemes.
He drinks from barrels of salty brew,
And tells tall tales of fish he knew.

With each gusty wind, he shouts with glee,
As his parrot squawks, "Hey, look at me!"
His compass spins; it always plays,
Hide and seek on foggy days.

He bumbles about with a creaky leg,
Missing the dock—oh, what a beg!
But with a grin, and laughter bright,
He sails on, ready for the fight.

So here's to sailors, wild and free,
With hearts of storms, we laugh with glee.
As waves crash, and storms may start,
Each journey holds a funny heart.

Dreams Drift with the Tide

A crab in a tux, dancing with glee,
Waves tickle his toes, oh, what a spree!
Fish gossip in bubbles, a shimmering crew,
Sunny sunbathers yell, "We want a view!"

Sandcastles sprout like mushrooms on shore,
While seagulls squawk, "We want much more!"
A dolphin does tricks, tails make a splash,
As beach balls zoom, it's a beachy bash!

Mermaids throw parties with glitter and light,
Clams sing their songs, what a silly sight!
The tide rolls in laughter, a jolly parade,
Every wave brings a joke, never to fade!

So come take a plunge in the water so bright,
Where dreams twist and twirl, a pure delight!
The sun sets, painting the sky with a start,
As laughter echoes, the waves play their part!

Cradle of Deep Blue Whispers

Bubbles pop softly, secrets they tell,
Octopuses giggle, casting a spell!
Urchins wear hats that wobble with glee,
As seaweed dances, quite wiggly-free!

Jellyfish juggle, a translucent show,
While fish in bow ties steal the front row!
Anemones cheer, waving arms in delight,
As conch shells hum tunes that wane into night!

Starfish and sand dollars play hide-and-seek,
With a wink and a wave, they're whimsical freaks!
Seashells spin stories of maybes and was,
While crabs chuckle hard at their own little flaws!

So dip your toes in, join this grand quest,
In the cradle of whispers, life's truly the best!
With every bubble, a chuckle or two,
This deep blue delight always welcomes you!

Waves of Secrets

Surfboards on the beach, they gossip and grin,
As waves roll in whispers, let the fun begin!
The tide tickles toes, says, "Join the parade!"
While sandcastles giggle in shimmering shade!

Seagulls fly overhead, with a sarcastic squawk,
Stealing fries from picnickers, oh, what a talk!
The sea turtles waddle, with swagger and grace,
While jellyfish jive in this quirky place!

A crab wears sunglasses, looking quite cool,
Sipping a drink at the beachside pool!
Hiding from prying eyes in a seaweed cloak,
He laughs at the splash of a sneaky old bloke!

With every wave, secrets slip and slide,
The beach holds laughter, so come for the ride!
Here, fun never ends, just laughs and high fives,
In these waves of silliness, everybody thrives!

Symphony of the Deep

In the depths where sea stars twinkle and hum,
A conductor fish waves, and the corals strum!
An octopus solo, tentacles in flight,
While a dolphin on drums makes the whole place ignite!

Clams on cymbals, they click and they clang,
A fin-tastic concert where sea critters sang!
With the bubbles as beats, and the currents as flow,
Every wave is a note in this whimsical show!

Squid paint the music, swirling in colors,
While flounders in tuxedos float like unbiased brothers!
Turtles sway gently, keeping the time,
While the seaweed swirls, a rhythm so prime!

So join in the fun where the sea meets the heart,
In this symphony deep, where laughter's an art!
With every splash and giggle, the joy never stops,
As friends in the deep share their love and their pops!

Moonlit Reflections on Water

Under the moon, fish dance and sway,
Jellyfish float like balloons in the hay.
Seagulls gossip with a cheeky flair,
Crabs tell secrets, well, if they dare.

Stars giggle as they peer from above,
Waves tickle toes, full of mischief and love.
Shells plot pranks in the moonlight's glow,
While seaweed sways with a cheeky show.

Frothy voices of surfers nearby,
Riding the waves, looking up at the sky.
Splashing about with laughter and shrieks,
A slippery whale speaks in clumsy tweaks.

So tiptoe softly, don't make a sound,
The ocean's silliness is all around!
Let's chuckle under the night's silver beam,
As fish wink at us, isn't it a dream?

The Salty Kiss of Evening

As day bids farewell with a salty salute,
Turtles wear shades, looking rather astute.
Crabs walk sideways, in stylish parade,
While dolphins giggle, their tricks home-made.

The sun dips low, in shades of bright gold,
Seashells share stories that never grow old.
Waves chase the sands, a game of tag,
Seagulls squawk laughter, their wings in a rag.

So raise your juice, toast the surf's jolly song,
As the ocean's whispers don't steer us wrong.
With every splash, we share a big grin,
In this salty embrace, let the fun begin!

As twilight laughs and fish start to bop,
The tide rolls in, and we laugh 'til we drop.
Mermaids sing tunes in sparkly delight,
While octopuses play chess, truly a sight!

Selkie's Embrace

On the shores where legends nestle and dream,
Selkies play tricks with a mischievous gleam.
With a wink and a splash, they wiggle away,
Leaving behind laughter, brightening the day.

They tease the fish, play tag in the foam,
Hooping and hollering, making the sea home.
Stars in their eyes, they dance on the tide,
Wearing seaweed crowns, with pride they abide.

A splash here, a giggle there, so profound,
Seashells collecting the joy that they found.
Every wave carries tales of their fun,
While the sun sets low, and the day is done.

So follow the laughter, let your heart roam,
In the salty embrace, we're never alone.
With selkies around, there's mischief at play,
Join in the antics, don't let joy decay!

Driftwood Tara

In the driftwood village where laughter does bloom,
Wooden figures gossip, making quite a room.
Clams wear tiny hats, it's a fashion parade,
While starfish play poker, waiting to trade.

The tides bring news, a quirky old tale,
Of mermaid escapades that never grow stale.
Waves crack jokes, they chuckle and roar,
Swishing the sands while they tumble ashore.

Driftwood Tara sings with a voice made of cheer,
Her melody floats, it's the sea we revere.
Seagulls join in, with a squawk and a spin,
As fish form a conga, it's a sight to win!

So let's gather 'round, spin stories so bold,
In a land made of laughter, where adventures unfold.
With a wink and a grin, dance on the shore,
In driftwood delight, who could ask for more?

Breath of the Sea

A fish wore a hat, thought he was grand,
He danced on the waves, thinking he'd planned.
But a seagull swooped low with a wink of his eye,
And off went the hat, oh my, oh my!

The jellyfish giggled, they bounced with delight,
While crabs on the shore prepared for a fight.
But one tripped on seaweed, fell flat on his back,
And laughter erupted—what a silly act!

A starfish was juggling old shells in a ring,
But the tide played a trick; it made them all fling.
They landed on sailors, who thought they'd been rocked,
And off went their bowler hats—what a shock!

So here by the shore, where the waves like to tease,
We find all the critters put on quite the sneeze.
They laugh and they play, in their watery spree,
With splashes of fun, just wait and see!

Echoes of Salt and Sand

In a conch shell, a clam sang a tune,
Claimed he was famous under the moon.
But when he hit high notes, the crabs all fled,
It's tough to be cool when you're full of dread!

A dolphin wore glasses, wanted to read,
But mistook a flipper for a book, oh indeed!
He flipped through the pages, oh where was the plot?
Got lost in a tale of a big, glowing yacht!

A turtle in shades was a self-proclaimed star,
He rode on a surfboard, said, "Look at me, para!"
But his pace was so slow; the waves passed him by,
"Fast is a turtle?" he'd dare to defy!

Shells giggled on the sand, what a funny crew,
Each whispering tales of the things that they knew.
From sandcastles grand to fish in a dance,
This playful parade sure knows how to prance!

Ballad of the Endless Deep

A whale with a smile and an oversized grin,
Tried to teach fish how to dance on a fin.
But one little guppy got tangled in sea,
And shouted, "Oh whale, why don't you just flee?"

An octopus chef had a cooking show,
Juggling sea cucumbers, throwing in dough.
But the batter exploded, krill flew like stars,
And fish swam away, quite miffed at his bars!

A crab with a toaster made breakfast for all,
He burned the seaweed, and it set off a squall!
"Breakfast is served!" he announced in delight,
While sea turtles roared, "This will cause quite a fight!"

But laughter erupted; they ate with great glee,
With gooey delights from the depths of the sea.
Each seafood shindig held flavors unique,
In this wave of humor, we find what we seek!

Currents of Forgotten Dreams

A fish with a dream to fly high in the air,
Took lessons from gulls, had them all in despair.
He flapped with such fervor, but only flopped down,
The discus of water, became quite the clown!

A starfish made wishes on glittery nights,
Hoping to become an elusive sea kite.
But winds were not favorable, stuck in the sand,
He mumbled, "Being lazy, I had not planned!"

A sea turtle thought he could be a great knight,
With a shell for a shield, oh what a sight!
But he met a fierce crab who wanted a duel,
And lost in the contest, felt rather a fool!

Yet they chuckled together, made peace with a dance,
In the currents that flowed, they found their own chance.
With bubbles and laughter, their tales intertwined,
In the depths of the sea, joy's what they defined!

Translucent Tales of the Deep

Bubbles rise like giggles free,
Fish swim past, what do they see?
A crab in shades, quite a sight,
Waves of laughter, pure delight.

Jellyfish dance, their wobbly show,
"What's your name?" asked the clownfish, "Do you glow?"
With tentacles flailing, the jellyfish replied,
"I'm just here to bring silliness as a guide."

Seahorses prance in a merry parade,
Telling tales of adventures they made.
"Did you hear about the turtle so sly?"
He wore sunglasses and tried to fly!

Starfish grinning on rocks like clowns,
Tickle these reefs, forget your frowns.
Life beneath waves, a laugh-out-loud scene,
In this watery world, all's light and serene.

Anemone's Prayer

An anemone waits with arms spread so wide,
"I'm not just a home, but a seaweed slide!"
With clownfish here, they giggle and squeak,
"Together we dance, though I'm rather meek!"

Shrimp nearby with a mischievous grin,
"Look at me bounce; I'm the jester of fin!"
The anemone chuckles, "You bring a good cheer,
Just watch for the eels; they love a good leer!"

Tangled in laughter, the seaweeds sway,
"Is it snack time yet?" a seagull would say.
But the anemone shouts, "Not food, friend of mine,
Join the fun and let's sip on some brine!"

So beneath the waves, where silliness reigns,
Creatures unite without any chains.
In the heart of the reef, where friendship is warm,
Life is a jest, a nautical charm!

Beneath the Starry Deep

Stars twinkle brightly in the murky blue,
"Wish for some bubbles!" calls a fish crew.
"Or maybe a treasure, shiny and gold,
Or a snail with a hat, oh, that would be bold!"

Crabs start a party, with pinch and prance,
"Join in the fun, come take a chance!"
With shells for drums and seaweed as tunes,
They dance like the tide, by the light of the moons.

A dolphin arrives with a splash and a flip,
"Let's race to the reef, take a slippery trip!"
With laughter and splashes, they zoom side by side,
In this starlit ballet, oh, what a wild ride!

Beneath the vast surface, where giggles reside,
Life is a story, and joy is the guide.
From the sand to the stars, camaraderie blooms,
In silliness found in the ocean's vast rooms.

Riptide Rhapsody

Riptides are swirling, oh what a jest,
"Hold on tight, it's a wild sea quest!"
With a splash and a giggle, they whirl around,
"Let's race the waves, where fun can be found!"

Octopuses juggle with ten arms afloat,
"Look at me, partner, I'm quite the boat!"
As starfish cheer with a flip of a flap,
"Hang on, hold tight, don't take a nap!"

Seagulls complain, "Hey, don't steal my fries!
Diving for snacks or would-be surprise."
Under the waves, where the currents don't sleep,
A symphony plays in the depths of the deep.

So come join the laughter, let's dance on the tide,
In the heart of the whirl, be you brave or wide-eyed.
Riptides may pull, but we'll swing and sway,
In the watery chaos, we'll surely play!

Tidal Harmony at Dawn

The seagulls squawk a silly song,
As morning waves roll right along.
Crabs in jackets, dancing neat,
Tap their claws to the ocean's beat.

Starfish in shades, lounging wide,
Trusting the tide, with shells as pride.
Sandcastles laugh, they tremble and sway,
'Look at us!' they cheer, 'We're here to play!'

Jellyfish waltz with a squishy glide,
While fish in bowties take the tide.
And dolphins joke with flips and turns,
As the sun wakes up, the fun still burns.

Waves tickle toes on the sandy shore,
Giggling seashells call for more.
The playful tide hums a light refrain,
A funny start to a day so plain.

Where Sea Meets Sky

Clouds wear hats, they float so high,
Birds trade jokes as they pass by.
The sun peeks out with a cheeky grin,
Lighting up waves like a playful din.

Surfboards spin, a wild dance,
The surfers catch every chance.
A crab in a trucker cap does a wheelie,
While mermaids giggle, oh so freely.

Fishes flip and splash for fun,
Twisting tales until they're done.
Oysters gossip, pearls on display,
As seaweed twirls in a funny ballet.

And as the sun starts to set,
Creatures chuckle, no hint of regret.
For every wave that chases ashore,
Is laughter echoing forever more.

Reveries of the Ocean Floor

A clam tells tales of treasure and gold,
While sea cucumbers act quite bold.
Octopuses juggle with eight clever hands,
In a circus of coral, where laughter expands.

Mermaids knit with strands of seaweed,
Crafting hats for fish with great speed.
Anemones wave, a colorful crew,
Tickling the toes of turtles passing through.

The hidden realms of the deep sea nest,
Where every creature attempts its best.
Shark in a bowler hat takes a break,
Munching on seaweed, a big, funny cake!

And down below, in the blue so bright,
Whimsical laughs echo day and night.
For in this realm of bubbles and glee,
The ocean's laughter flows boundlessly.

The Dance of Water and Wind

Wind tickles the waves, a playful tease,
Making fish shiver and sea birds sneeze.
The sun sports shades, looking quite cool,
As boats bob along in the sailor's school.

Kites swoop low, with laughter they dive,
Mixing with seagulls, both feel alive.
Wind whispers jokes to each passing swell,
And the water giggles, 'Oh do tell!'

Surf has a surfboard, stylish and neat,
Riding the breeze with rhythmic feet.
Riptides are busy washing away drab,
While waves crack jokes on a watery tab.

At the shore, the fun never fades,
Where laughter and tides form wild cascades.
So dance with the breeze, let silly times start,
And embrace the cheerful waves from the heart.

Depths of Tranquility

Bubbles rise with a giggly glee,
Fish are laughing, can't you see?
Seaweed dances, a wobbly jig,
Crabs in tuxedos, oh so big!

Seagulls squawk in a wild game,
Chasing waves, they're never tame.
Starfish pose, they strike a pose,
Splashing water, they spill their prose.

Sunken treasures on the sea floor,
Mermaids playing hide and score.
Turtles tripping, a wobbly race,
As jellyfish giggle, what a place!

Underwater, the party's bright,
With dancing plankton, pure delight.
Crashing waves with a hearty laugh,
Nature's circus, it's quite the craft!

The Secrets of Shipwrecked Souls

Ghostly pirates play a prank,
Arguing over a treasure bank.
With eyepatches come silly faces,
Searching for their lost shoe laces!

Skeletons in a dance-off, sway,
Booty shaking, come what may.
Cannons whistle a merry tune,
While sea turtles lounge, quite immune!

Buried secrets beneath the tides,
A treasure map that just divides.
With every twist, a pouting fish,
Who'd rather munch than grant a wish!

Mermaids tease from the coral throne,
Whispering tales in a playful tone.
"Hope you brought snacks for this ride!"
As shadows run and giggles abide!

Sails and Sunglasses

Captain's hat and shades so bright,
Sailing east into the light.
With squirrels stowed in the cabin's nook,
Ready for an oceanic cook!

Gulls steal snacks, they're quite the thieves,
As laughter sails upon the breeze.
Seashells chat with the sun-kissed sand,
In nautical wonder, oh isn't it grand?

The wind is playful, tugging at strings,
And dolphins join in on silly flings.
"Don't capsize!" warns a wise old seal,
As we roll and sway, oh what a deal!

Waves clap hands, "Join the fun!"
Under the sun, we're never done.
So raise your cups to the salty cheer,
With sails and shades, the world's sincere!

Horizons of Hope

Painted skies at the break of day,
Balloons float, in a silly play.
With a wink, the sun starts to shine,
While jellybeans dance across the brine.

Friendly whales sing a bouncy beat,
As crabs tap toes to a sandy sheet.
Dolphins leap through the colors bright,
Their giggles echo in mere delight.

Sunset's glow brings a cheerful swirl,
Every wave gives a twirling whirl.
Paddleboats racing, a puppies delight,
Under the stars, our dreams take flight!

Let's chase horizons, bold and true,
With every laugh, adventure anew.
In the fun realm where spirits soar,
The heart of the sea forever will roar!

Romance of the Riptide

A wave once winked at a passing fish,
It said, "Come here, fulfill your wish!"
But the fish just splashed, and swam away,
Leaving the wave in a bubbly fray.

Seagulls laughed as they flew above,
"Oh look, that wave's in love!"
They dipped and dived with glee in the blue,
While the wave just swirled, feeling quite blue.

A crab in sunglasses sat on the shore,
Hollering, "Stay calm and surf some more!"
But the wave just rolled with a silly pout,
Hoping to find what it was all about.

In the end, the sunset bathed it in gold,
The wave chuckled softly, "I'm already sold!"
And with every splash, a new romance,
The tide will rise for one more chance.

Secrets Beneath the Sea Spray

Bubbles giggled through salty air,
Whispers of secrets, oh, what a pair!
A starfish strolled in the shimmering light,
Said, "I've got tales that are out of sight!"

A turtle with shades joined the fun,
"Did you hear the one about the big, tasty bun?"
All the fish swam close to confess,
Their jokes made the sea seem much less serious!

A clam with a pearl offered a clown,
"Why don't crabs ever play around?"
The crowd laughed hard, "We don't know why!"
"Because they're always caught in a pinch," said the guy!

As the waves danced with each sprightly tease,
Secrets floated like leaves in the breeze.
With laughter echoing throughout the deep,
The sea kept its secrets, but joy it would keep.

Sirens' Echoes at Dusk

As dusk fell over the shimmering bay,
Sirens sang songs that made sailors sway.
Each note was sweet, but oh, what a trick!
When they'd lure a boat, it'd happen so quick!

One sailor danced, thinking he was grand,
Till he stumbled and fell right out of the sand.
"Swim faster!" the shouts from the ocean rang,
But he laughed, "Don't worry, I can just clang!"

With bubbles and giggles, the sirens played games,
Mimicking words like they were fish names.
"Bubbles McSwimmy! Come quick!" they would yell,
While sailors just laughed, under their spell.

At the break of dawn, when the laughter ceased,
The echoes faded, but not the feast.
With fish on their plates and tales turning bright,
The dawn brought a chuckle 'til the next night!

The Rhythm of the Gentle Waves

The waves tapped a beat on the sunlit sand,
While crabs danced their dance, a curious band.
"Join us!" they beckoned, but I shook my head,
"Last time I tried, I ended up spread!"

Seashells giggled as they rolled to and fro,
"Come join our concert, we'll steal the show!"
The rhythm was catchy, like a soft lullaby,
Even the dolphins swayed as they brushed by.

A flotilla of fish formed a line to parade,
Wiggling and jiggling, a fin-tastic charade!
The seaweed waved like it knew all the moves,
While the sun winked down, caught up in the grooves.

As night fell gently, stars joined the song,
The ocean whispered, "You've belonged all along!"
With moonlit mischief and laughter so brave,
Under the sky, we all swayed with the waves.

Crashing Waves of Memory

In a boat of cupcakes, we set sail,
Forgot the paddles, but we won't fail.
The seagulls laugh as they swoop down,
Stealing our snacks, wearing crowns of brown.

With every wave comes a splash of cheer,
Bouncing our laughter, it's all crystal clear.
We dance on deck like fish out of line,
Silly sea shanties, our voices combine.

A dolphin flips, wearing sunglasses cool,
Says, "Join the party! That's the rule!"
We dive for treasure, only find old shoes,
But who needs gold when we've got the blues?

Bubbles in laughter, we ride the foam,
Every wave whispers of the joy of home.
So here we be, in a salty delight,
Chasing the sun, sailing to the night.

Depths of Reflection

In blue-green waters, we search for gems,
Finding lost socks and old pairs of hems.
A crab waves back, it's quite the affair,
Clearly, it's seen better days of hair.

The mirror-like waves reflect our muse,
Making funny faces, we cannot lose.
A starfish laughs as it wiggles close,
Says, "Life's a dance, so let's all dose!"

We stumble and tumble in a splashy fling,
Our shouts of glee resonate and sing.
Down here it's quirky, at times absurd,
Saltwater soap starts bubbling, quite stirred.

So grab a friend, let's dive in quick,
In this watery world, let's learn a trick.
To dance with the fish, let worries go,
And ride on the currents in a funny flow.

The Tide's Gentle Touch

The tide rolls in, new friends abound,
Shells all giggling, on the sandy ground.
We build a castle with moats of glee,
While a crab tries on our hats for free.

The waves tickle toes, oh what a prank!
We're seeking treasures, giving thanks.
A seaweed hat, a crowning delight,
Bobbing our heads, we dance with the light.

Seashells sing when they catch the breeze,
Making up jokes, like "Why did you freeze?"
"Because I'm a clam!" said the shell with pride,
We laugh so hard, we nearly slide!

As the sun sets down, painting the sky,
We wave goodbye with a funny sigh.
Tomorrow we'll come, let the waves play their part,
For each tide that comes, brings light to the heart.

Shipwrecked Whispers

Lost at sea in a barrel of laughs,
We're pirates now with fun-loving gaffs.
A parrot squawks, "You can't steal my cheer!"
While juggling coconuts, we shed a tear.

Flotsam and jetsam, our treasures galore,
A rubber ducky and a rusty door.
We toast with coconuts to all we've found,
While a mermaid does cartwheels, quite unbound.

The seaweed sways to our pirate song,
"Who needs maps when you just go along?"
With every splash, we giggle and shout,
Our shipwreck's a party—renewed without doubt.

So here we'll camp on this deserted isle,
With laughter echoing a nautical style.
For shipwrecked whispers are full of delight,
Chasing dreams in the stars, we'll sail through the night.

Guiding Stars over Waters Deep

At night the fish all throw a dance,
With twinkling lights that seem to prance.
They twirl beneath the moon's cool glow,
While jellyfish just steal the show.

A crab in shades takes center stage,
With fancy moves that turn the page.
He tries to surf on a passing wave,
But ends up stuck—what a funny knave!

The turtles cheer with flippers wide,
As seagulls joke and their feathers glide.
A dolphin's leap, a big surprise,
Turns into belly-flops—oh, what a prize!

And just beneath the silent tide,
Clams chuckle softly, full of pride.
With every splash, the ocean's cheer,
Makes waves of laughter, oh so near.

Celestial Currents

Up in the sky, fish stars align,
They line up well, it's quite divine.
A seaweed twirl, a foam-filled chase,
Turns into laughter, a joyful race.

The octopuses play hide and seek,
With eight long arms, they never peak.
A walrus sings a silly tune,
While fishermen dance under the moon.

The tides are like a perfect prank,
As surfers tumble in the tank.
With splashes that go whoosh and splat,
They giggle more than a silly cat!

As bubbles rise to the ocean's top,
Fish just can't help but laugh and flop.
Among the waves, a comical sight,
The sea's a stage, oh, what delight!

Whispers of the Salty Breeze

Along the shore, the seagulls squawk,
Spreading tales of fish gone for a walk.
The tide rolls in with a clumsy trot,
As barnacles chatter, linking the plot.

A starfish sunbathes on the rocks,
Dreaming of fancy boxy socks.
While hermit crabs swap their old homes,
Shuffling fast, they giggle in foams.

The sea cucumber jokes about its fate,
While pondering if it's truly late.
A wave says, "Hey! You look so fine!"
While sardines dance in a shiny line.

With salty air that fills the laugh,
Each little fish has earned a plaque.
In this vast world of funny tunes,
The sea embraces all its loons!

The Horizon's Embrace

The horizon calls with a friendly grin,
Where mermaids swim and the tales begin.
With giggles and splashes, the coral grows,
As neighbors wink from their hidden shows.

A fish in a tux, so dapper and neat,
Sways to the rhythm of the ocean's beat.
While sea snails race with shells on their backs,
They laugh like kids in colorful tracks.

Dolphins flip and wiggle with glee,
Making waves, oh so carefree.
While clowns of the sea, the porpoises leap,
In an aerial show that's never steep.

Under the waves, the humor thrives,
As every splash keeps the ocean alive.
With jokes and jests beneath the blue,
The horizon smiles, its joy shines through.

Dance of the Seafoam

Bubbles rise and fall with glee,
Waves do a jig, oh can't you see?
Starfish tap their tiny feet,
While seagulls croon a silly beat.

Sandcastles tumble, it's quite the show,
Crabs are dancers in a row.
Flip-flops dance as they drift around,
With laughter echoing, joy abounds!

Jellyfish twist in a gleeful trance,
Their tentacles flail in a silly dance.
Laughter ripples through the foam,
As fish join in, they're not alone!

Gulls are clowns with a honking sound,
While dolphins leap, they spin around.
What a party on the shore,
Where fun and splashes always roar!

Whispers in the Nautical Night

Stars above giggle in delight,
As crabs compete in a moonlit fight.
Gull's cawing echoes, sounds so bright,
While fish debate who's out of sight.

Sailboats sway like they're in a trance,
As waves do a wiggly dance.
The whispers of the sea are clear,
Full of secrets, laughter, and cheer.

Octopus paints with a splashy flair,
Adding colors with crafty care.
Turtles chuckle, racing along,
As starfish sing a comical song.

In the night, they share a tale,
Of fishy fables and winds that wail.
With giggles and snorts, the sea unites,
In this nocturnal, joyful flight!

Beneath the Moonlit Waters

Beneath the waves, what a sight to see,
A clam in ballet is quite the spree!
His shell does twirl 'round and 'round,
Making all the other fish astound!

Seaweed sways like it's in a play,
Starfish applaud in their own way.
A whale floats by with a puzzled look,
Wondering about this underwater book.

Dolphins peek, with giggles that soar,
As turtlenecks wear jackets, oh what a score!
They strut and laugh, full of delight,
In this whimsical world, oh what a night!

Algae disco lights twinkle and gleam,
An underwater party, like a dream.
With scrappy fish that tease and tease,
The moonlit waters are full of ease!

Lament of the Tide's Embrace

Oh tide, why do you pull and sway?
So many shells want to stay and play!
But you roll them back to salty deep,
While laughing at the memories they keep.

Oysters grumble, with a clammy frown,
Why do you push them all around?
"Just let us rest!" they squawk and plead,
But the tide's quirkiness won't concede.

A fish with charisma, wearing a tie,
Tries to negotiate, oh me, oh my!
"Let's form a band, a tide-beyond!"
But the tide just chuckles, waving fond.

So they float, and bob, in a comical plight,
As the tide huffs and puffs, feeling quite light.
In this playful wrestle, all is good cheer,
For laughter fills the waves, far and near!

Symphony of Silent Waves

The fish all dance in their tiny jeans,
While crabs form a band with their clattering claws.
A dolphin giggles plotting naughty schemes,
As seaweed sways and the snail takes a pause.

The starfish plays guitar on a sandy stage,
With seagulls clapping, it's quite the affair.
A turtle joins in, though he's slow with age,
And jellyfish float with electric flair.

A whale sings deep, but it's off-key a bit,
The shrimp roll their eyes; they'll never give in.
While barnacles join for a quick little skit,
They laugh till they cry, in their shells made of tin.

So come take a dip where the antics abound,
In this underwater show of pure delight.
Where laughter and bubbles echo around,
And even the sea foam is sparkling bright.

Murmurs in the Moonlight

The crabs in tuxedos go waltzing around,
While clams hold their pearls in a dazzling spin.
A sea otter juggles a rock he has found,
It's quite the odd talent; he laughs with a grin.

The seaweed whispers, 'What's cooking tonight?'
While fish in a chorus sing songs with a twist.
They'll brew up a storm with their sea-foam delight,
A frothy concoction you surely can't miss!

The moon winks down with a mischievous glow,
As dolphins plot pranks on the unsuspecting.
They'll leap and they'll splash, put on quite the show,
While seahorses blush at their own silly jesting.

So let's dance and twirl as the waves serenade,
With bright little bubbles to pop with our cheer.
We'll sway with the tides in this wild escapade,
Laughing in unison, no worry or fear!

Song of the Siren's Cradle

In the depths, ocean folk prepare for a feast,
With mermaids serving cake made of sea foam and sand.
The seagulls complain, they've been left out at least,
They squawk and they squabble, it's all rather grand.

A nautilus sings with a voice so divine,
While clowns of the sea pull a prank on a ray.
An octopus juggles, it's simply sublime,
With a wink and a wave, he'll steal your bouquet.

A party ensues, the eels twist and shout,
While fish form a conga, they're leading the way.
A blowfish inflates, though it's all for a clout,
Yet somehow he smiles in his silly display.

So come for a dive, bring your giggles and cheer,
The sea's full of magic, it's hard not to laugh.
Where bubbles abound, it's a jubilant sphere,
And laughter's the currency that brings joy in half!

Secrets Beneath the Surface

A clam tells a tale of the time he was bold,
He straightened his shell and sported a hat.
The fishes all gasped, 'What a sight to behold!'
As bubbles of laughter swirled round where he sat.

Anemones giggle, their tickles a breeze,
While a flounder struts with a grin ear to ear.
The humor is thick as the plankton with ease,
As seagulls on shore just wipe off a tear.

In the sun's gentle rays, they all share their jokes,
With whales providing the bass, oh so low.
The jellies do flips, and the sea otters poke,
Keeping the rhythm in waves of bright flow.

So dive down below, where secrets arise,
And laughter is stitched in the very sea floor.
For creatures of waves, with their mischievous cries,
Bring joy to the depths and so much more!

www.ingramcontent.com/pod-product-compliance
Lightning Source LLC
Chambersburg PA
CBHW060115230426
43661CB00003B/196